BEN'S BIG BOOK OF
CARS

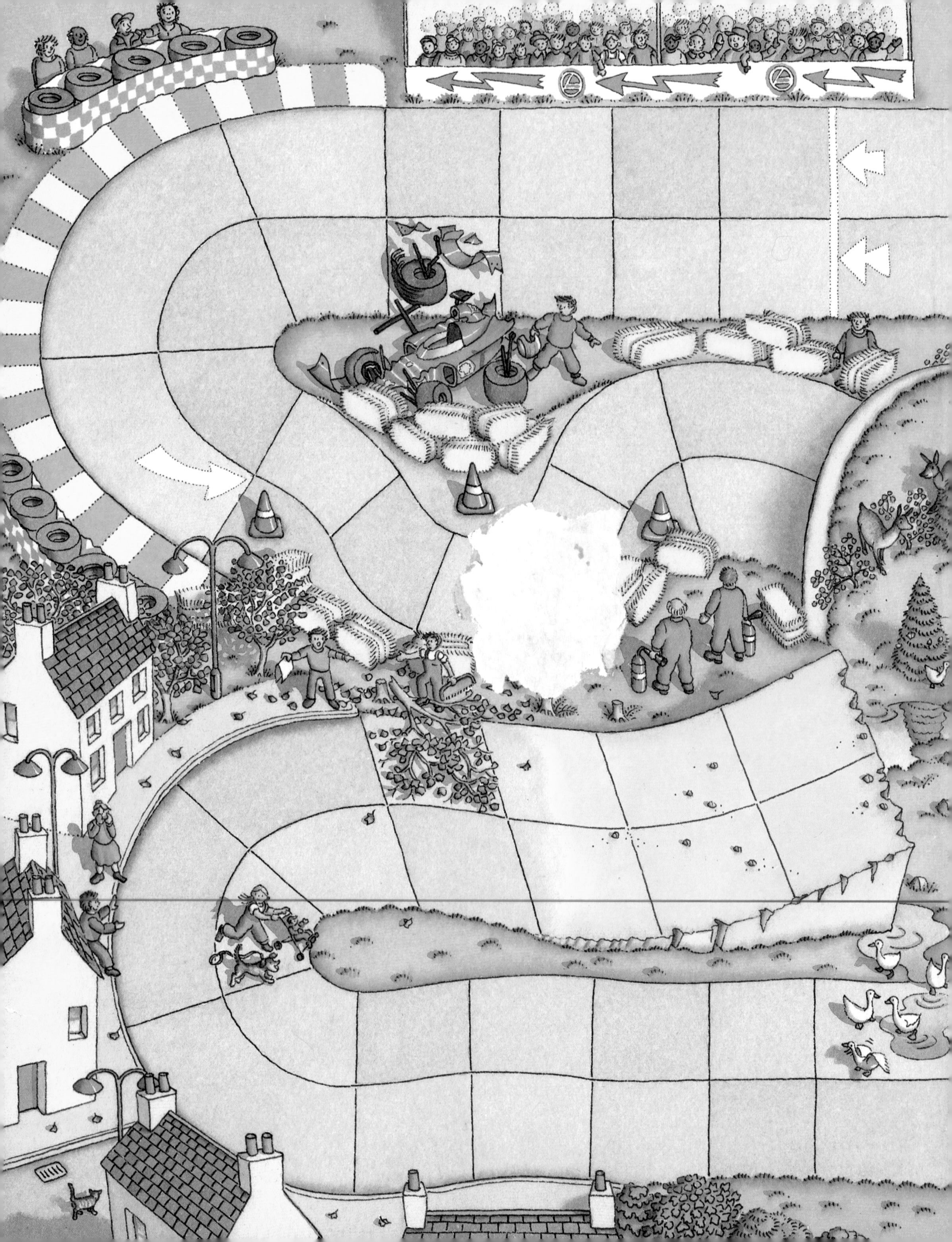

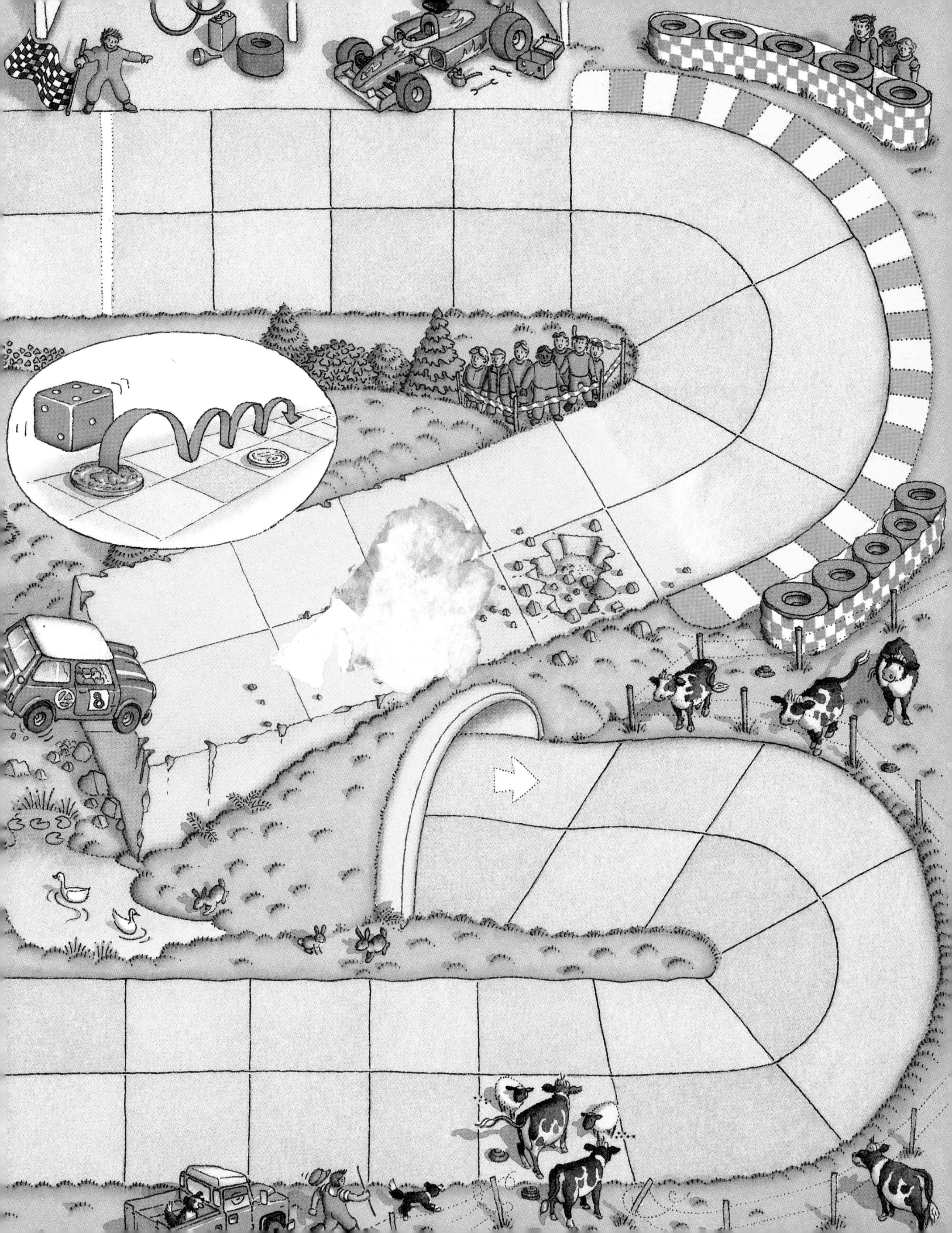

For Harry Hendy Butcher

BEN'S BIG BOOK OF CARS
A RED FOX BOOK 0 09 940472 9

First published in Great Britain by Hutchinson,
an imprint of Random House Children's Books

Hutchinson edition published 2002
Red Fox edition published 2003

3 5 7 9 10 8 6 4 2

Red Fox Books are published by Random House Children's Books,
61–63 Uxbridge Road, London W5 5SA,
a division of The Random House Group Ltd,
in Australia by Random House Australia (Pty) Ltd,
20 Alfred Street, Milsons Point, Sydney, NSW 2061, Australia,
in New Zealand by Random House New Zealand Ltd,
18 Poland Road, Glenfield, Auckland 10, New Zealand,
and in South Africa by Random House (Pty) Ltd,
Endulini, 5A Jubilee Road, Parktown 2193, South Africa

THE RANDOM HOUSE GROUP Limited Reg. No. 954009
www.**kidsatrandomhouse**.co.uk

A CIP catalogue record for this book is available from the British Library.

Printed in Hong Kong

BEN'S BIG BOOK OF CARS

Ben Blathwayt

RED FOX

All Kinds of Cars
Three-wheeler
Two wheels at the back and one at the front
TIE 123
Saloon
A smart car to drive to work
People carrier
Enough seats for a big family
RED 010
Estate
Lots of room in the back
PIE
Van
For small deliveries and light loads

CRA554
HER 035
Four-wheel drive
The engine controls all four wheels
so it is easy to drive over bumpy ground
Hatchback
A smaller version of the
estate car
FTS007
Convertible
The roof can
go up or down
Pick-up truck
Strong enough for tough use
PTU
162
Sports car
Goes very fast!

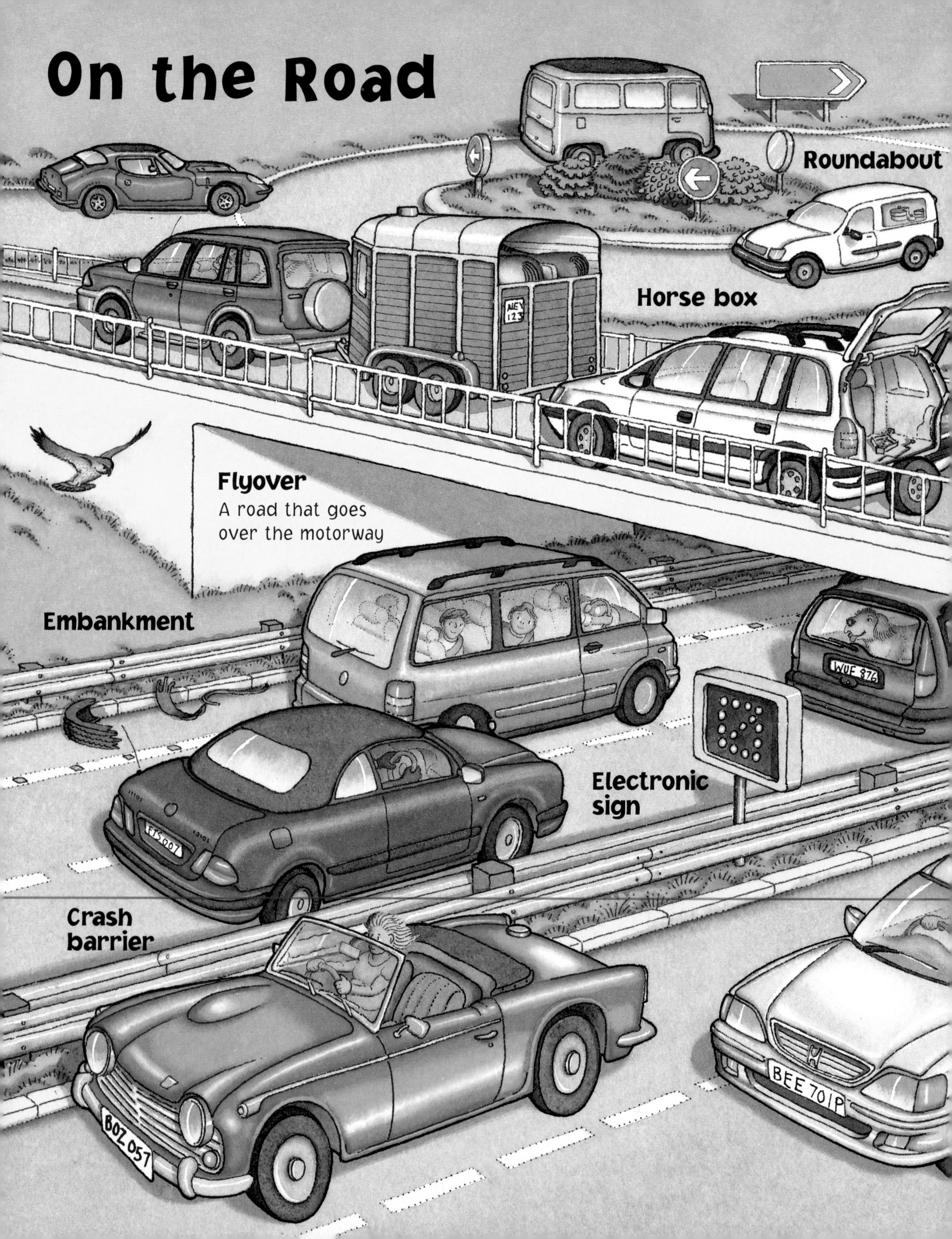
On the Road
Roundabout
Horse box
AEY 123
Flyover
A road that goes over the motorway
Embankment
WUF 876
Electronic sign
FJS 007
Crash barrier
BOZ 057
BEE 701P

Cattle bridge
Caravan
Police car
PCI 071
LALOO8
CRASS4
Emergency telephone
Hard shoulder
Cars can only stop on the motorway if they break down

Taking a Break

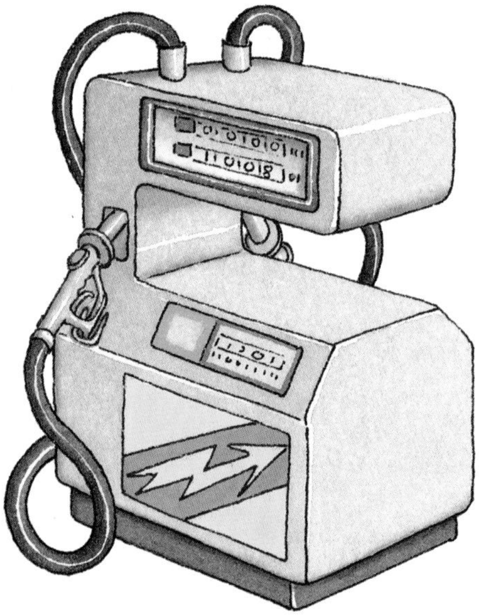

Fuel pump
To fill up the tank

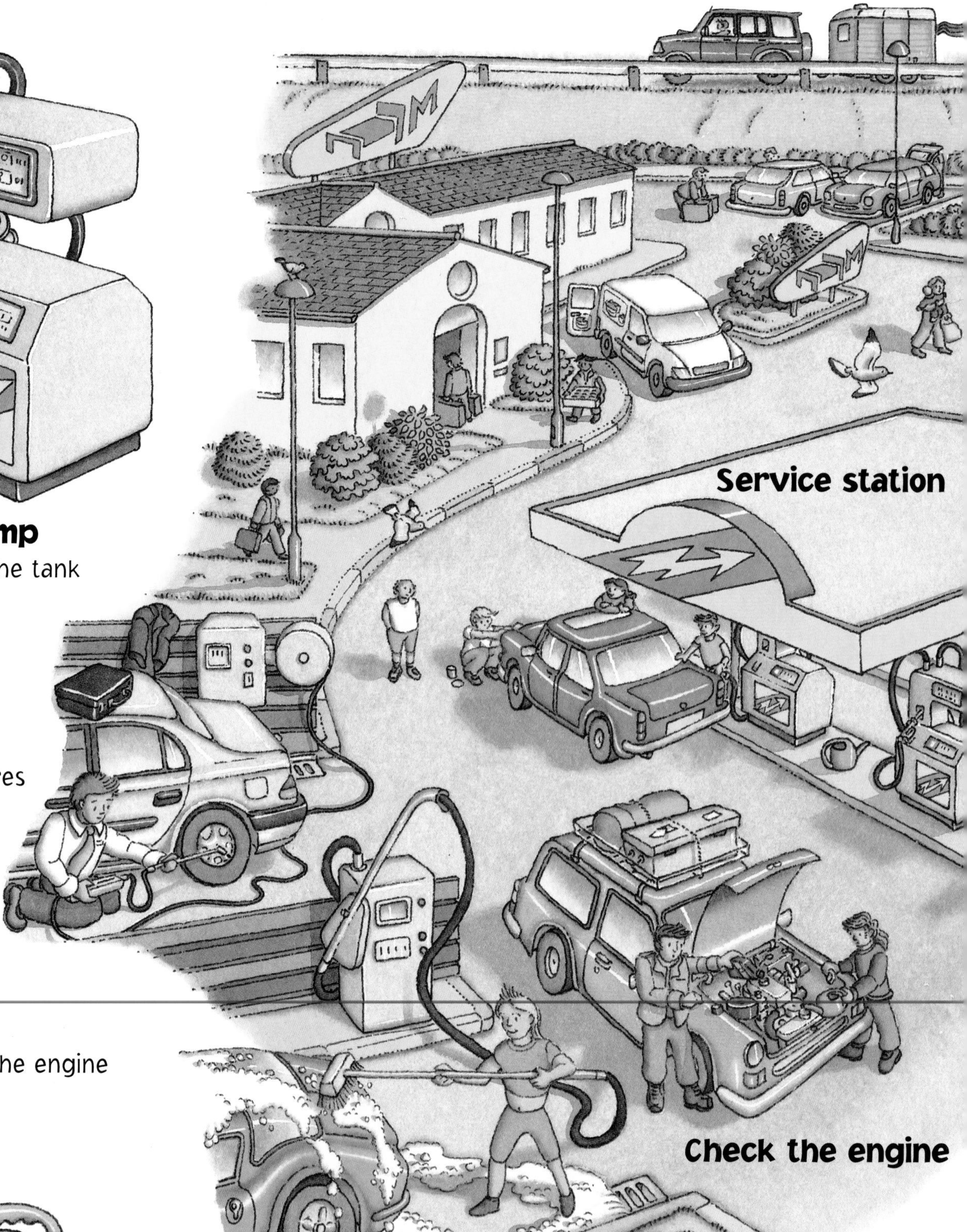

Air
For the tyres

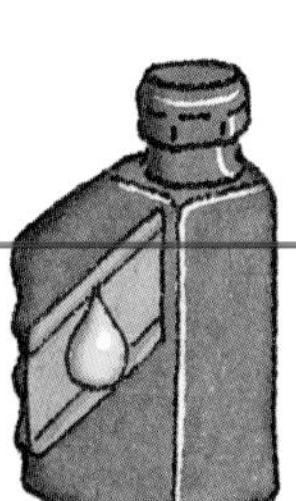

Oil
For the engine

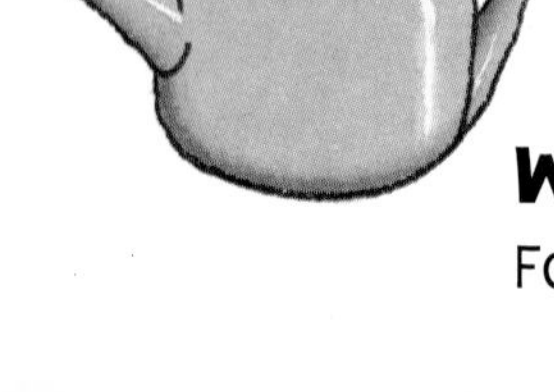

Water
For the radiator

Service station

Check the engine

Car wash
For a clean, shiny car

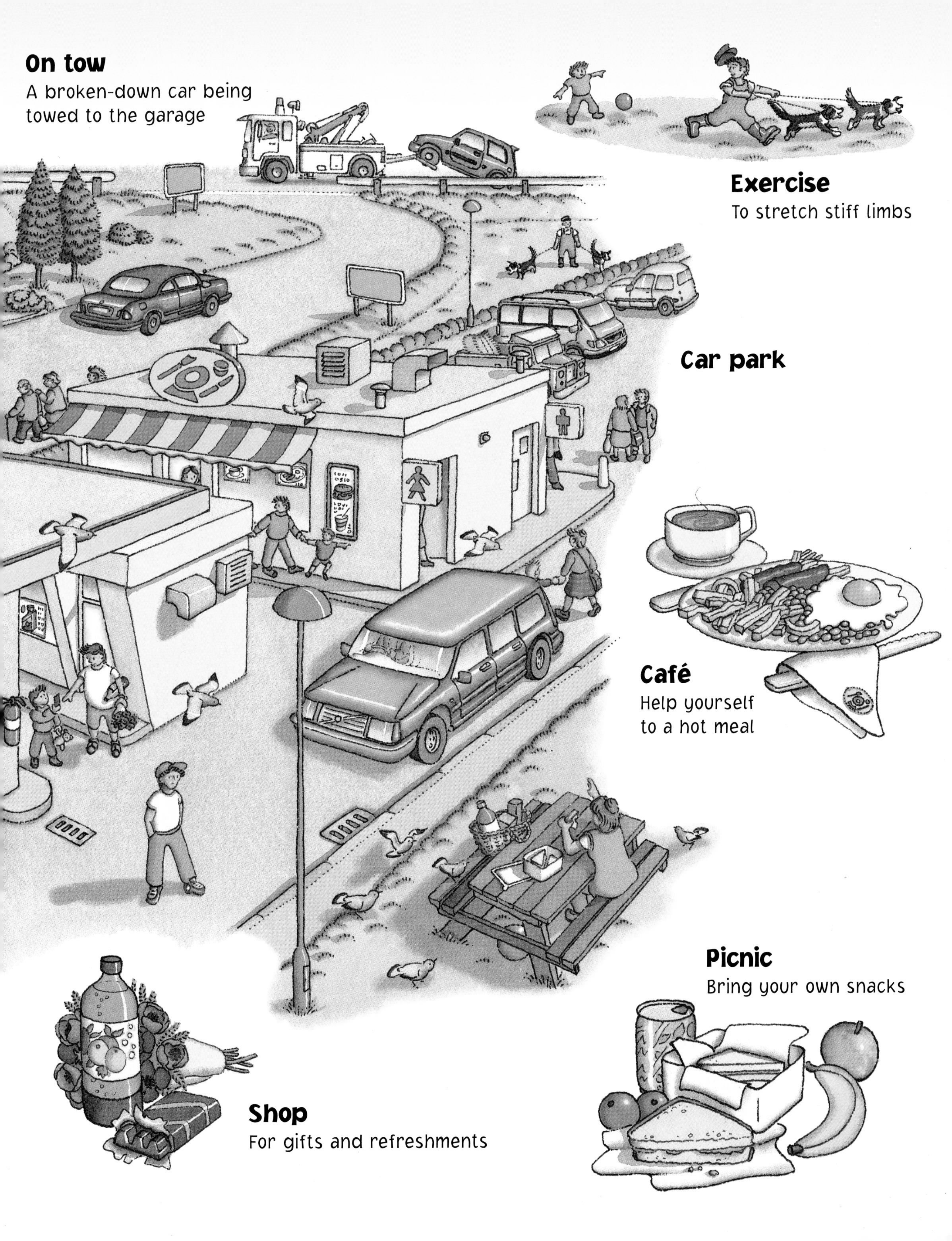
On tow
A broken-down car being towed to the garage
Exercise
To stretch stiff limbs
Car park
Café
Help yourself to a hot meal
Picnic
Bring your own snacks
Shop
For gifts and refreshments

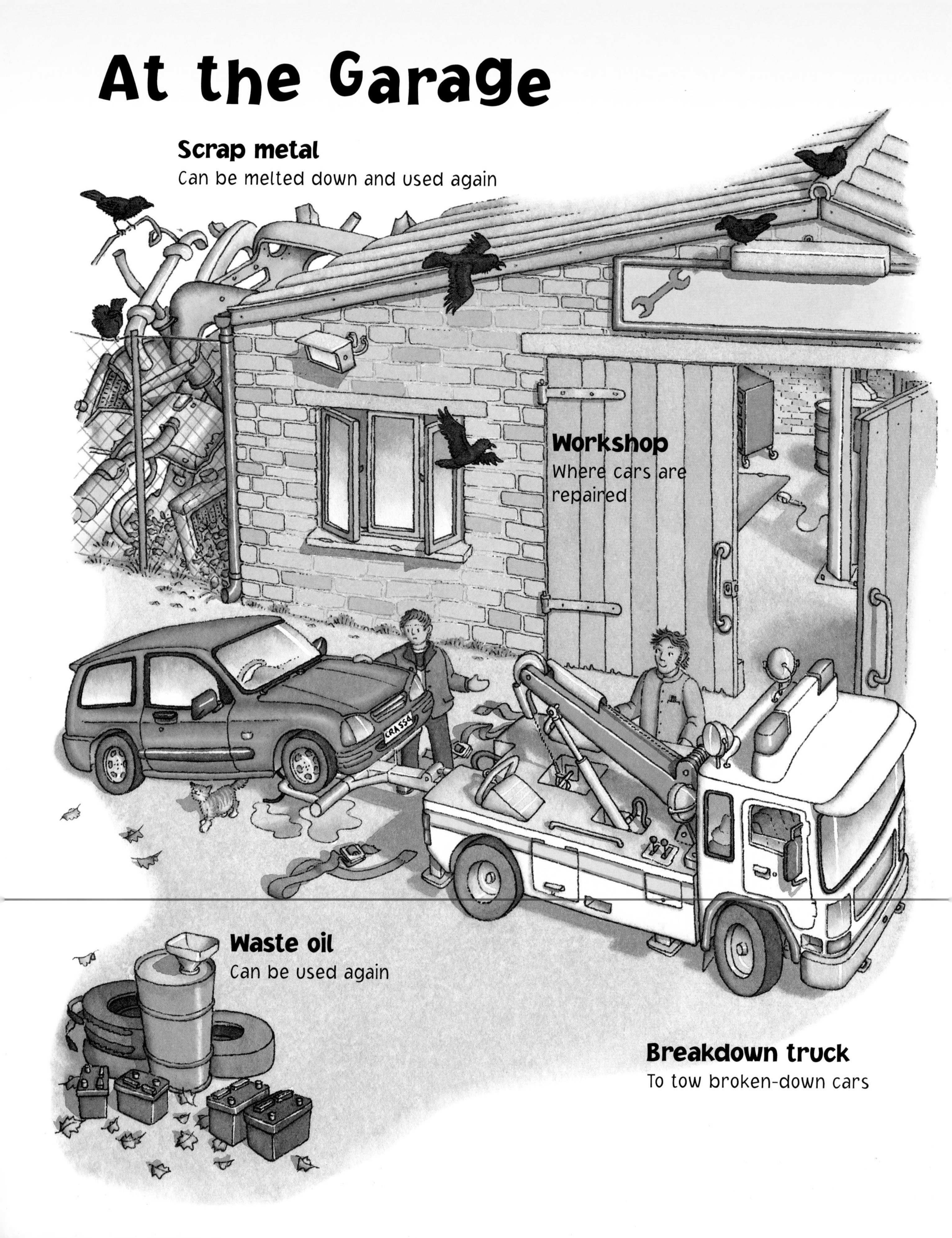
At the Garage
Scrap metal
Can be melted down and used again
Workshop
Where cars are repaired
Waste oil
Can be used again
Breakdown truck
To tow broken-down cars

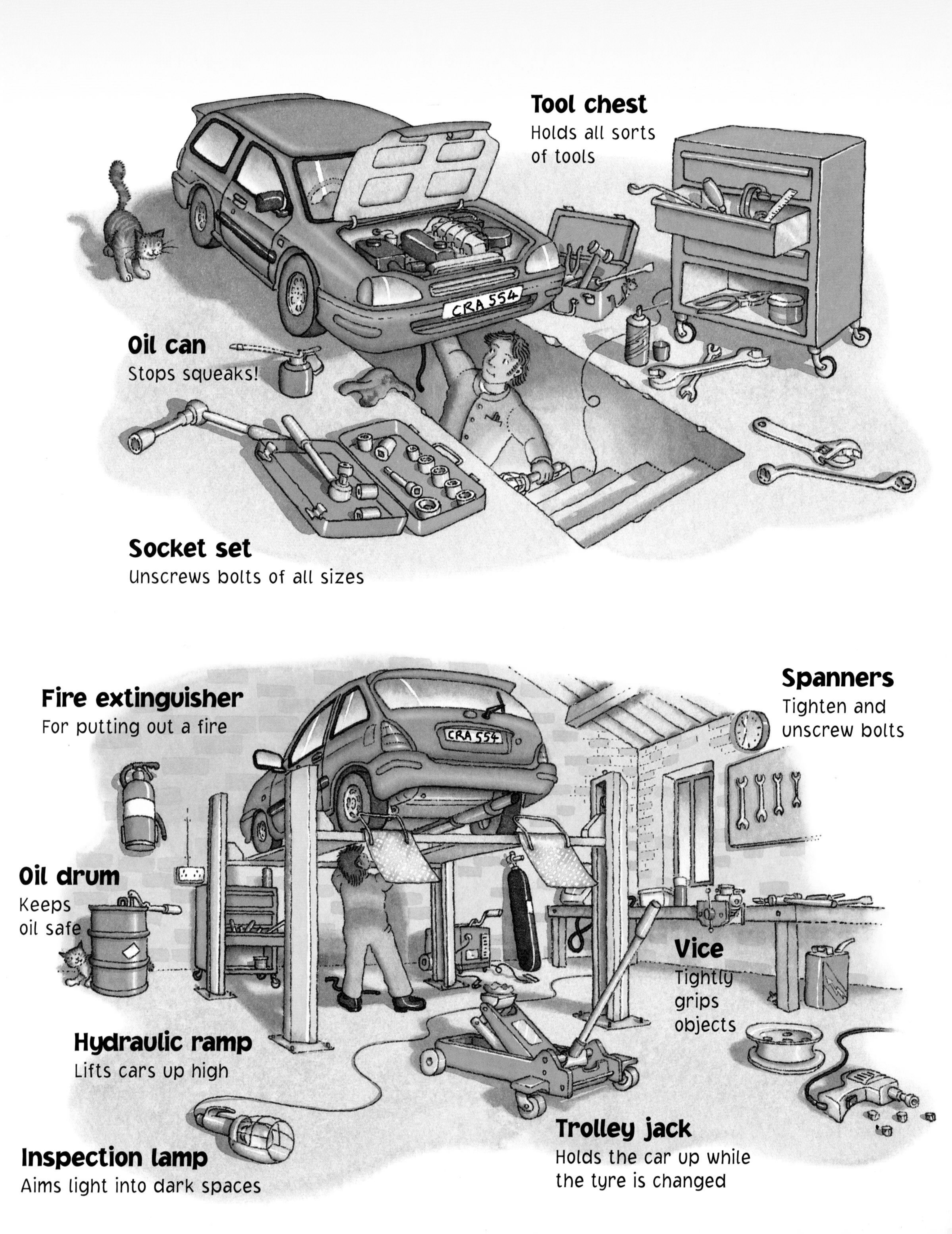
Tool chest
Holds all sorts of tools
CRA 554
Oil can
Stops squeaks!
Socket set
Unscrews bolts of all sizes
Fire extinguisher
For putting out a fire
Spanners
Tighten and unscrew bolts
CRA 554
Oil drum
Keeps oil safe
Vice
Tightly grips objects
Hydraulic ramp
Lifts cars up high
Trolley jack
Holds the car up while the tyre is changed
Inspection lamp
Aims light into dark spaces

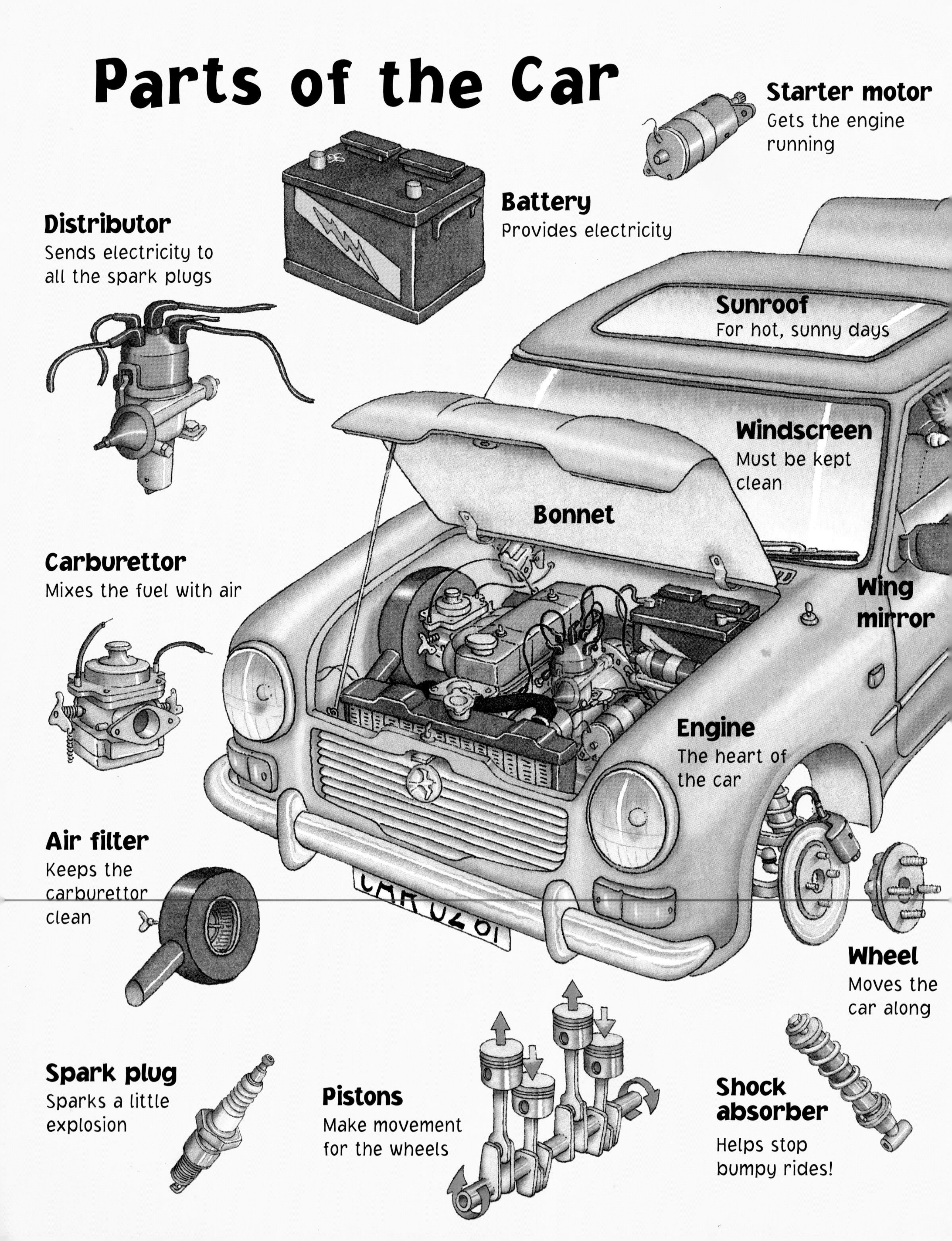
Parts of the Car
Starter motor
Gets the engine running
Battery
Provides electricity
Distributor
Sends electricity to all the spark plugs
Sunroof
For hot, sunny days
Windscreen
Must be kept clean
Bonnet
Carburettor
Mixes the fuel with air
Wing mirror
Engine
The heart of the car
Air filter
Keeps the carburettor clean
Wheel
Moves the car along
Spark plug
Sparks a little explosion
Pistons
Make movement for the wheels
Shock absorber
Helps stop bumpy rides!

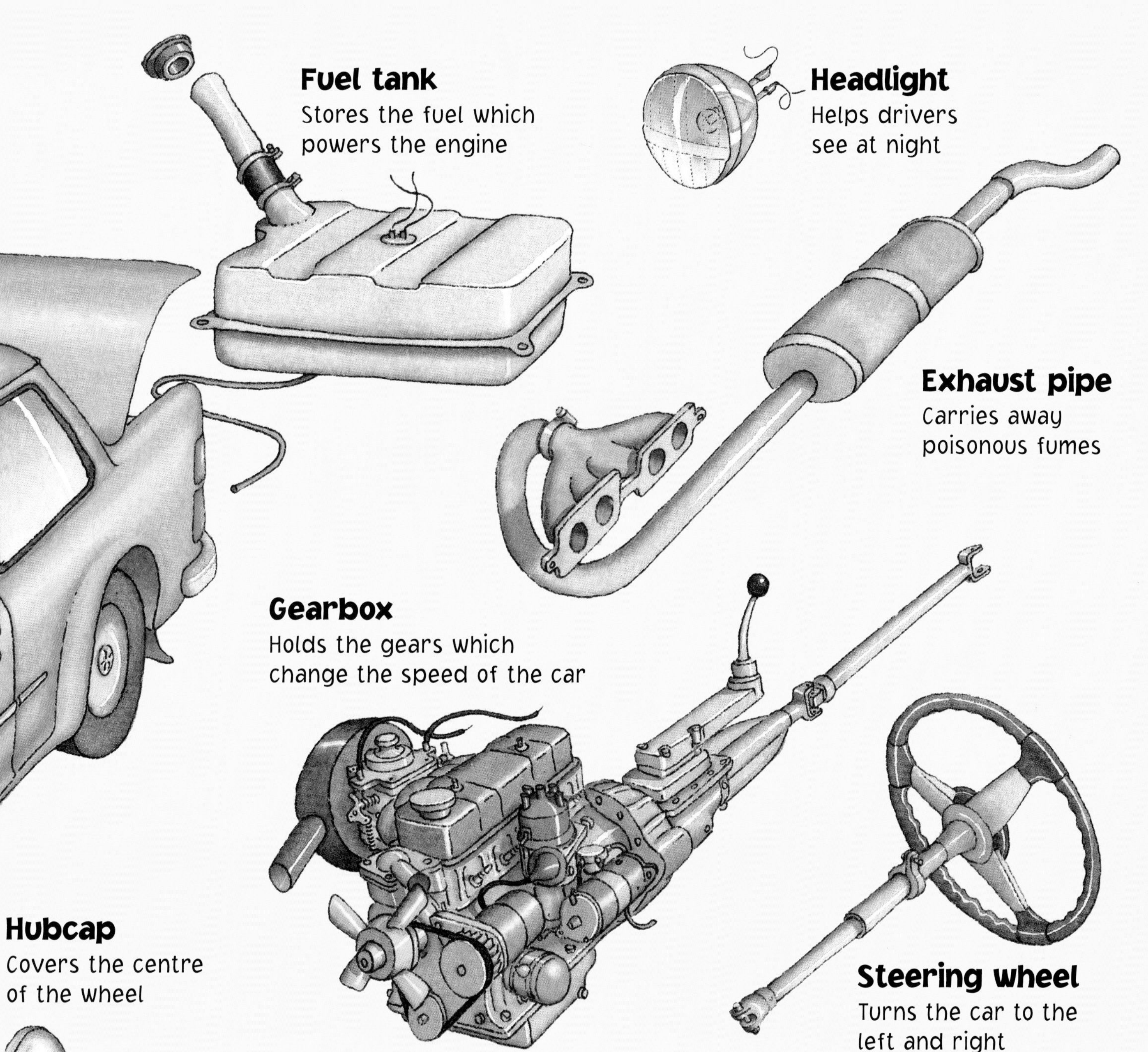

Fuel tank
Stores the fuel which powers the engine

Headlight
Helps drivers see at night

Exhaust pipe
Carries away poisonous fumes

Gearbox
Holds the gears which change the speed of the car

Steering wheel
Turns the car to the left and right

Hubcap
Covers the centre of the wheel

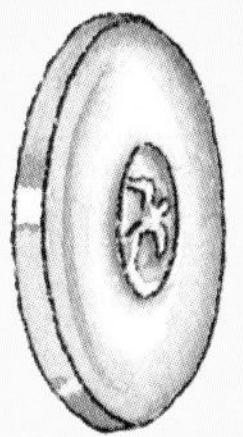

Disc brake
Slows and stops the car

Tyre
Grips the road and helps stop skidding!

Radiator
Cools the water that stops the engine overheating

First Cars

Panhard-Levassor, 1901

The Panhard-Levassor was one of the first cars to have an engine at the front, a gearbox, four wheels rather than three and a proper steering wheel.

Model T Ford "Tin Lizzie", 1908

Bugatti Type 35, 1924

Early cars were very expensive, difficult to drive and unreliable. In 1908 Henry Ford designed a car that everyone could afford. His factories produced over 23 million Model T Fords.

Some drivers wanted only speed and excitement from their cars, others were happy with comfort and reliability.

Rolls-Royce
Phantom II Continental, 1929

Cars that Race

Dragster
Very noisy and very fast

Go-cart
Small, low to the ground and lots of fun!

Stock car
Specially adapted for rough racing, these cars often crash!

Sports car
Sports car races can last a whole day and night

Touring car
Ordinary cars with specially tuned engines to make them go fast!

Rally car

Must be strong enough
for the roughest of tracks

Grand Prix racer

A magnificent racing
machine with a big engine,
big tyres and a long,
smooth body

Rally Car Racing

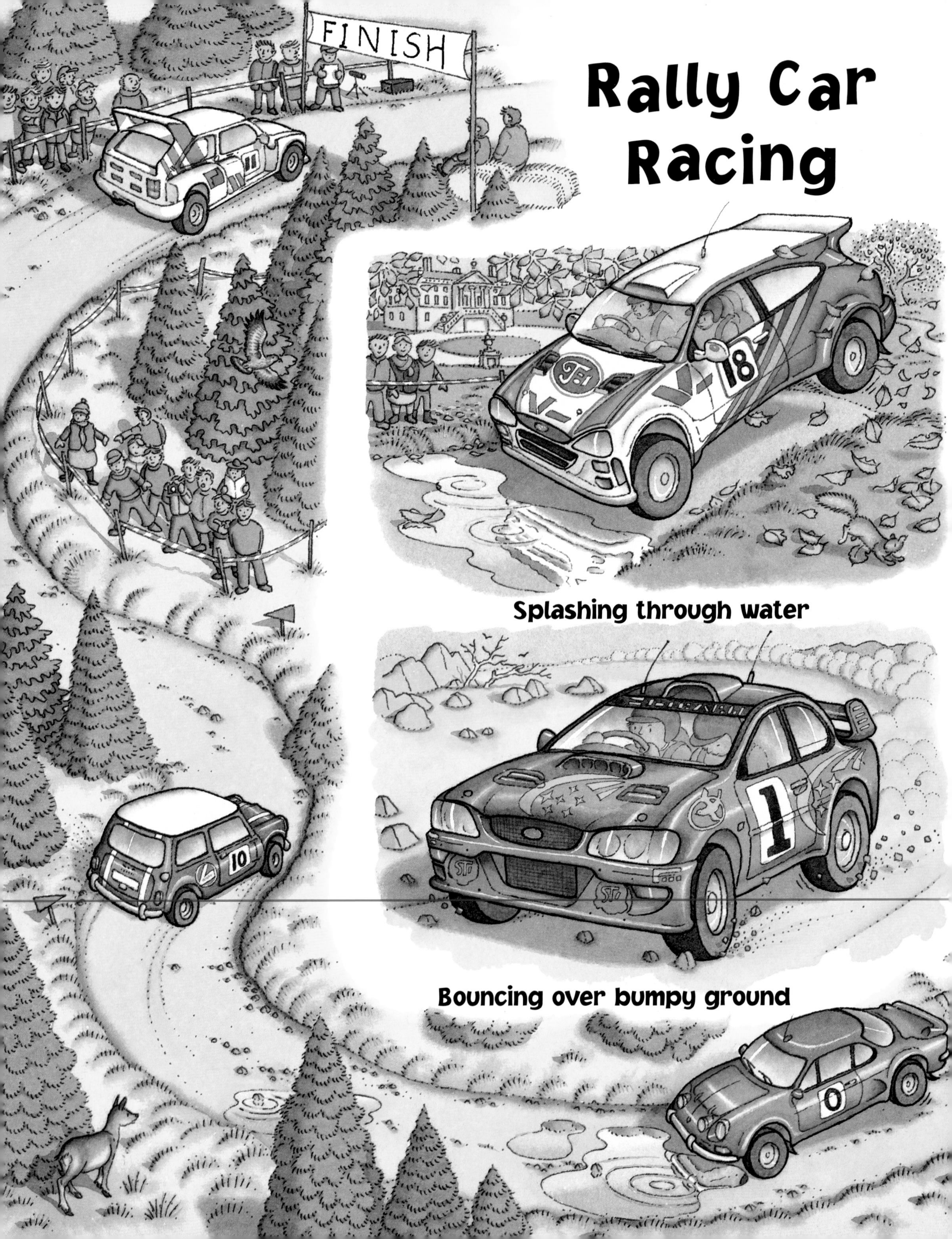

Splashing through water

Bouncing over bumpy ground

Rally cars race one by one over a course that is often narrow and rough. The fastest time wins!

Skidding on snow

Speeding round corners

Grand Prix Racing

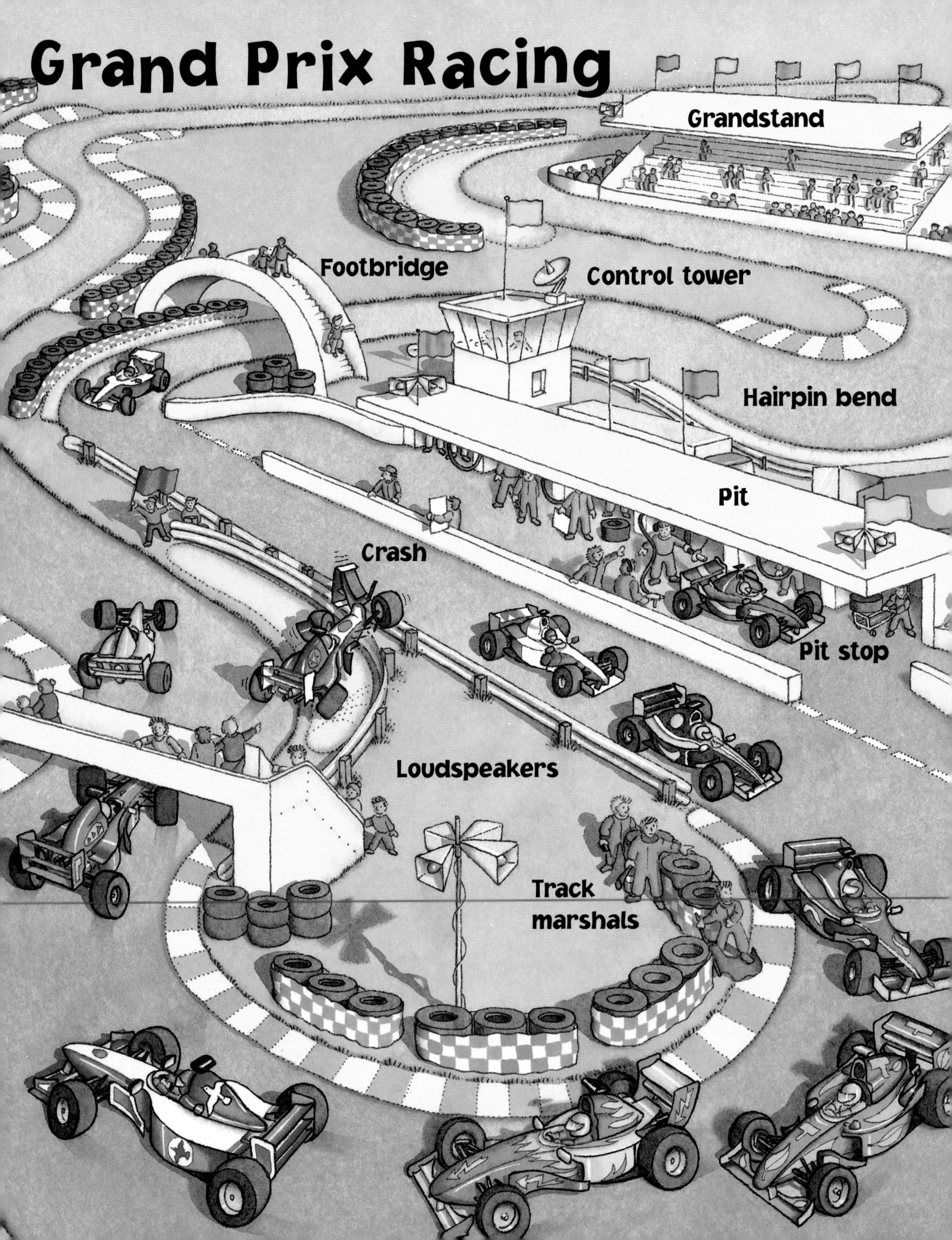

Getting ready to race

Out on the circuit

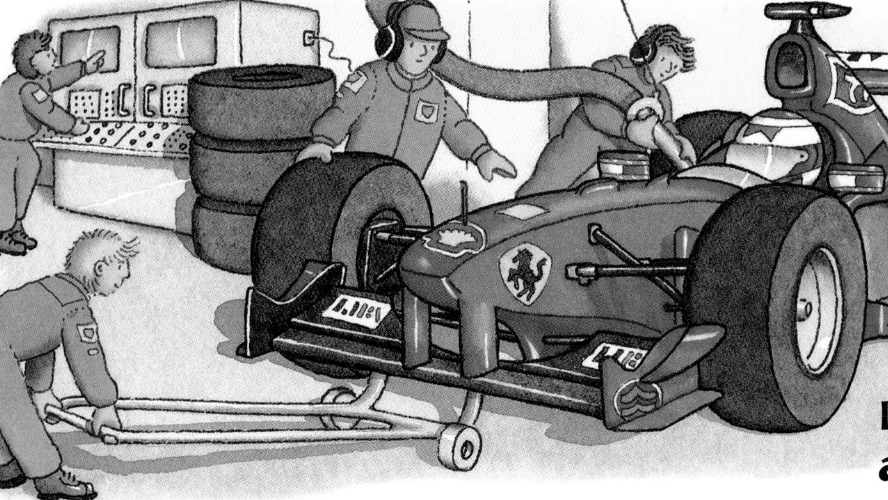

Into the pit for more fuel
and a quick tyre change

Super Cars

Lamborghini Countach
For very rich people!

Ferrari F40
One of the fastest cars in the world

Jaguar E-Type

Named after a wildcat

Morgan Plus 8

Every car is handmade

Porsche 911

Some people's dream car

Classic Cars

Popular in their day
and still seen on
the road today!

Morris Mini Minor
Very small and
easy to park

Volkswagen Van
The whole family can go on holiday

Volkswagen Beetle
Designed by Ferdinand Porsche

Austin Healey "Frogeye" Sprite
A classic British sports car

Citroën DS "Décapotable" (convertible)
Stylish, with a special suspension

Morris Minor

Very reliable

Morris Minor Traveller

Reliable with lots of room

SAAB 96

Designed for the cold Swedish winters

Ford Escort RS

Won lots of rallies in its time

Citroën 2CV "Deux Chevaux" (two horsepower)

Ideal for getting the wind in your hair!

Fiat 500 "Topolino" (little mouse)

A perfect, little, city car

Unusual Cars

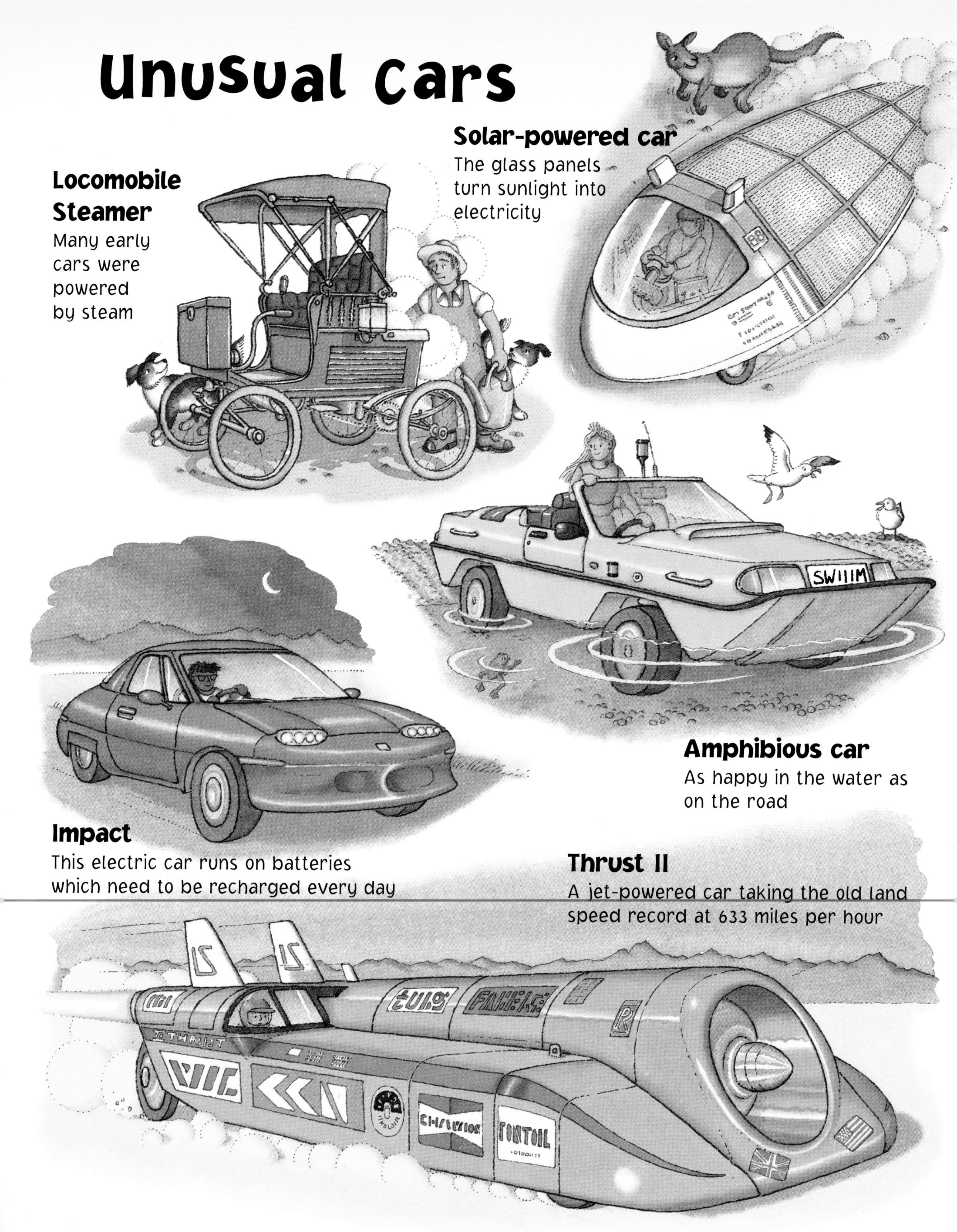

Locomobile Steamer
Many early cars were powered by steam

Solar-powered car
The glass panels turn sunlight into electricity

Amphibious car
As happy in the water as on the road

Impact
This electric car runs on batteries which need to be recharged every day

Thrust II
A jet-powered car taking the old land speed record at 633 miles per hour

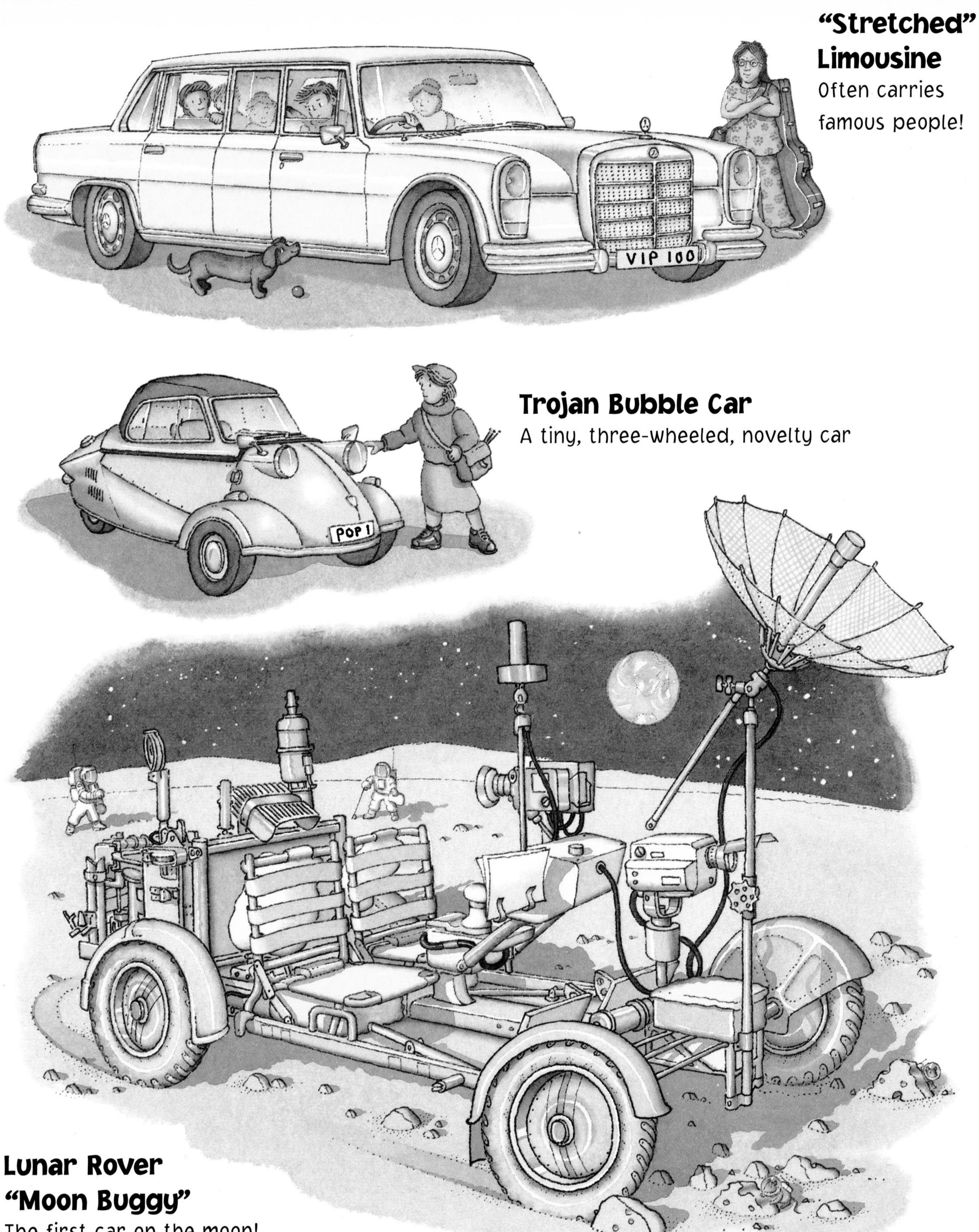

"Stretched" Limousine
Often carries famous people!

Trojan Bubble Car
A tiny, three-wheeled, novelty car

Lunar Rover "Moon Buggy"
The first car on the moon!

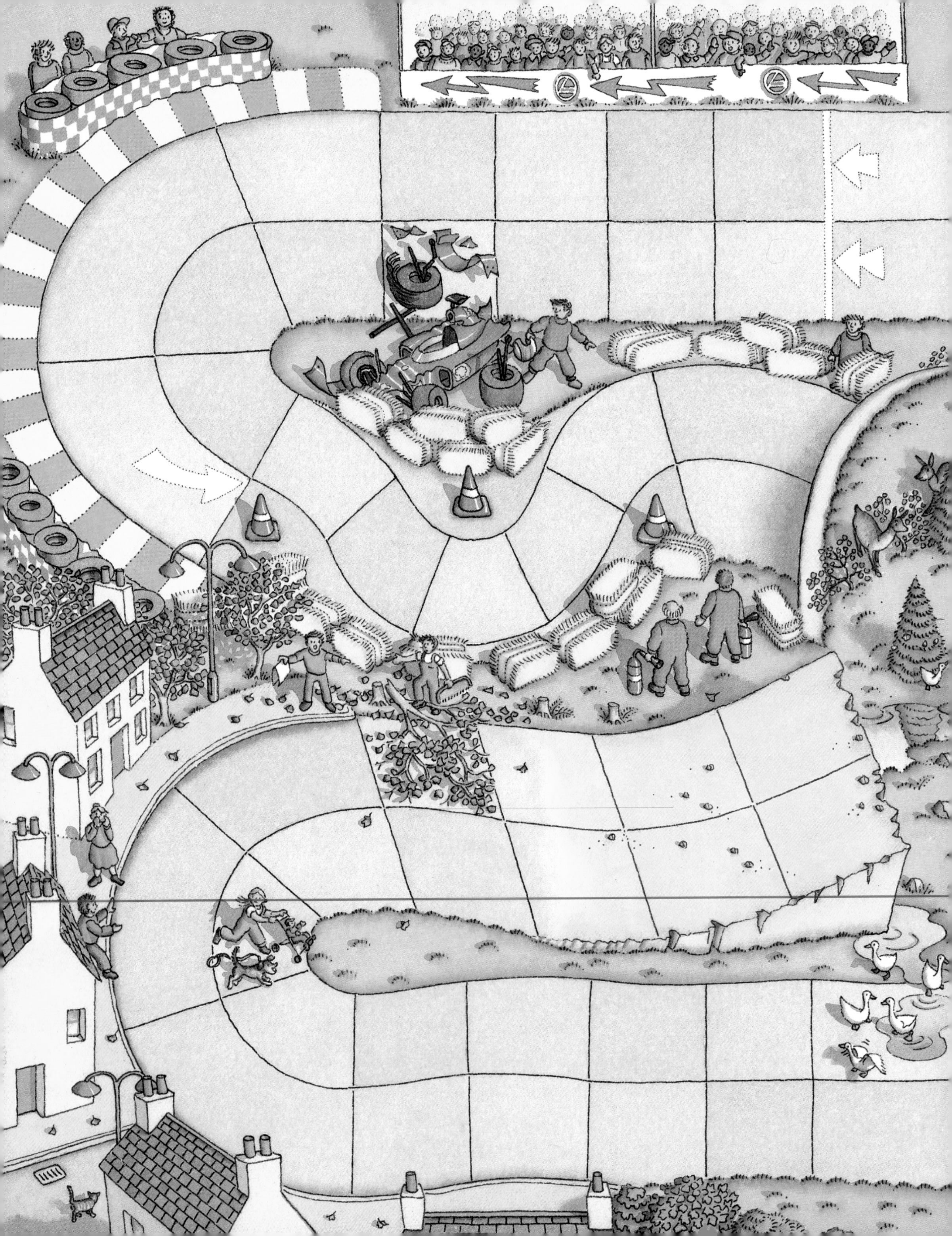

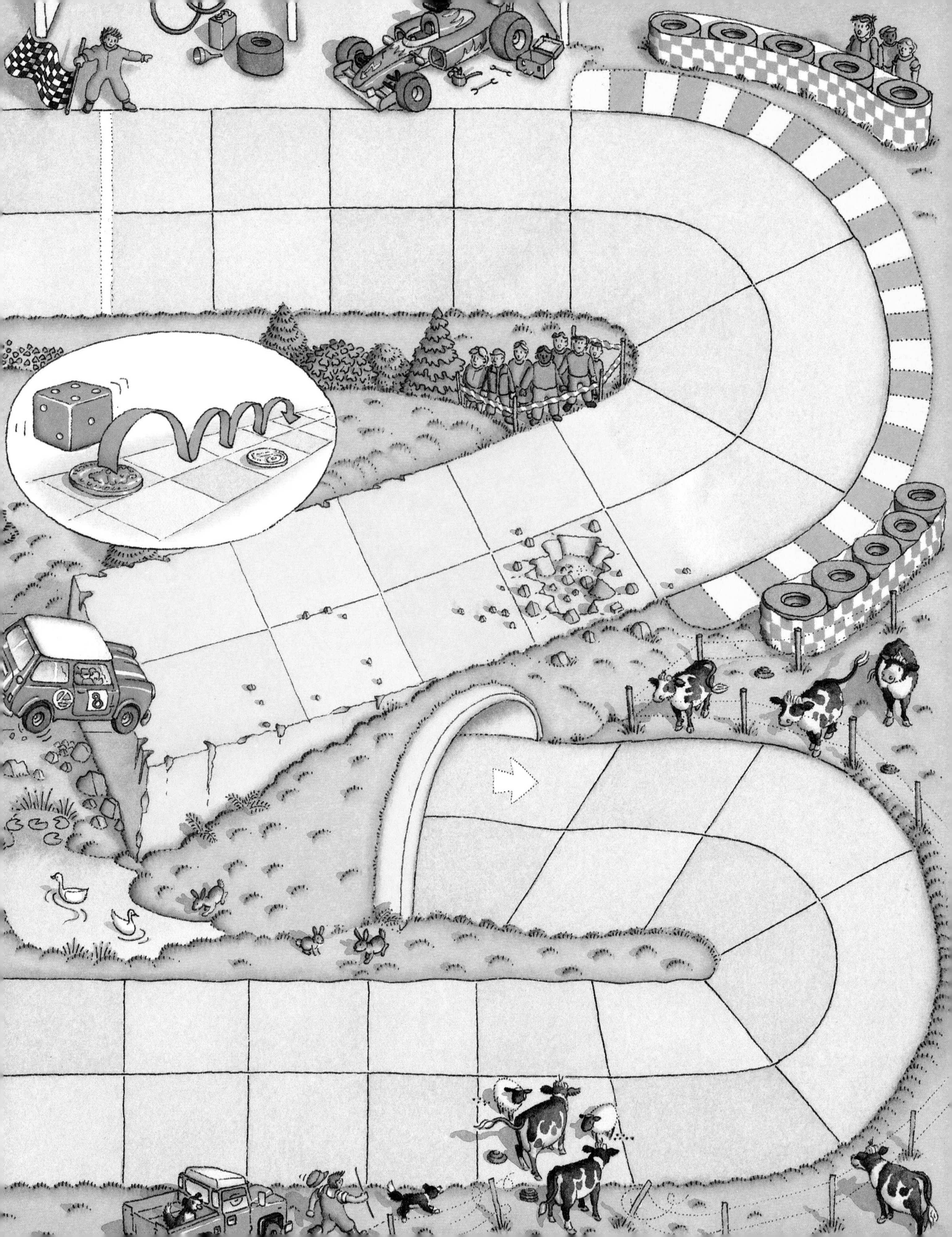

OTHER BOOKS BY BEN BLATHWAYT

The Runaway Train
0 09 938571 6

Little Red Train to the Rescue
0 09 969221 X

Faster, Faster Little Red Train
0 09 926499 4

Green Light for the Little Red Train
0 09 926502 8

One Farm
0 09 940759 0

BOARD BOOKS BY BEN BLATHWAYT

Little Red Train
1 85 681584 6

Yellow Digger
1 85 681674 5

Blue Tractor
1 85 681684 2

Aeroplane
0 09 176837 3

Ferry
0 09 176847 0

Rally Car
0 09 176867 5

Big Truck
0 09 176857 8